Earth

by Martha E. H. Rustad

CAPSTONE PRESS
a capstone imprint

Little Pebble is published by Capstone Press,
1710 Roe Crest Drive, North Mankato, Minnesota 56003
www.capstonepub.com

Library of Congress Cataloging-in-Publication Data
Rustad, Martha E. H. (Martha Elizabeth Hillman), 1975– author.
 Earth / by Martha E. H. Rustad.
   pages cm.—(Little pebble. Space)
 Audience: Ages 5–7.
 Audience: K to grade 3.
 Summary: "Simple text and full-color photographs describe Earth"—Provided by the publisher.
 Includes bibliographical references and index.
 ISBN 978-1-4914-8321-3 (library binding)—ISBN 978-1-4914-8325-1 (pbk.)—
ISBN 978-1-4914-8329-9 (ebook pdf)
1. Earth (Planet)—Juvenile literature. I. Title.
 QB631.4.R87 2016
 525—dc23   2015023307

Editorial Credits
Erika L. Shores, editor; Juliette Peters and Katelin Plekkenpol, designers;
Tracy Cummins, media researcher; Katy LaVigne, production specialist

Photo Credits
NASA: NOAA/GSFC/Suomi NPP/VIIRS/Norman Kuring, 9; Shutterstock: AstroStar, 5, cigdem, 7, Denis Tabler, cover, 1, Kalenik Hanna, Design Element, Lucian Coman, 19, momanuma, 17, Mopic, 11, PaulPaladin, 13, sebikus, 15, Sergey Novikov, 21

Editor's Note
In this book's photographs, the sizes of objects and the distances between them are not to scale.

Printed and bound in the United States of
America. 072018   000782

Table of Contents

Our Home

What is Earth?

A planet!

Planets orbit stars.

Planets are big and round.

Eight planets orbit the sun.

Earth is third from the sun.

sun

Mercury

Venus

Earth

Mars

Jupiter

Saturn

Uranus

Neptune

Earth is almost 8,000 miles (13,000 kilometers) wide.

9

Earth has three layers.

We live on the crust.

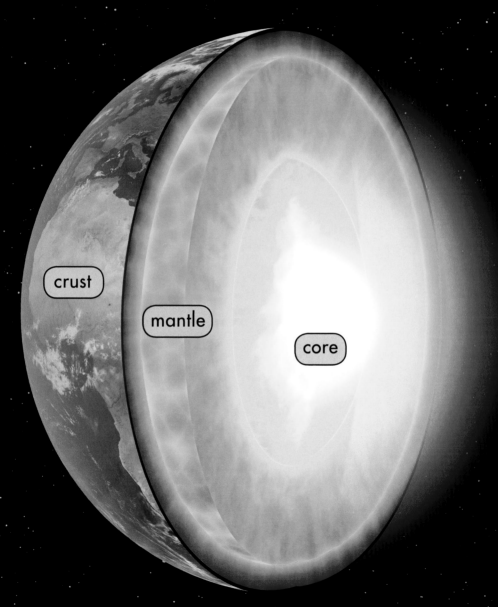

Moving

Earth spins each day.

The side facing the sun has day.

The other side has night.

sun

moon

Earth

Earth orbits the sun.

The trip takes one year.

Just Right

The sun warms Earth.

Earth is not too hot.

It is not too cold.

Plants and animals live
on Earth.

We have water to drink.

We have air to breathe.

Earth makes
a good home.

Thank you, Earth!

Glossary

breathe—to take air into and push it out of the lungs

core—the center; Earth's core is hot, liquid rock

crust—the outer layer

layer—a level of thickness that covers something

orbit—to follow a curved path around an object in space

planet—a large object in space that orbits a star

star—a ball of burning gases; the sun is a star

Read More

Bredeson, Carmen and Marianne Dyson. *Exploring Earth.* Launch into Space! New York: Enslow Publishing LLC, 2015.

Edison, Erin. *Sunlight.* Weather Basics. Mankato, Minn.: Capstone Press, 2012.

Roumanis, Alexis. *Earth.* Planets. New York: AV2 by Weigl, 2016.

Internet Sites

FactHound offers a safe, fun way to find Internet sites related to this book. All of the sites on FactHound have been researched by our staff.

Here's all you do:
Visit *www.facthound.com*
Type in this code: 9781491483213

Super-cool stuff! Check out projects, games and lots more at **www.capstonekids.com**

Index